# The Jets and the Rockets

Story by Jenny Giles  Illustrations by Rachel Tonkin

Luke and Andrew were out on the field with the rest of their class.
They were going to play baseball.

Baseball was their favourite game.
Luke played for the Jets,
and Andrew played for the Rockets.

Luke said to Andrew,
"My team is going to win today."

Andrew shook his head.
"No," he said. "We will win.
The Rockets always win."

"Not today!" said Luke.

Luke ran onto the field with the Jets.
The Rockets went to sit in a line.

Zoë was the first to bat.
The ball came towards her,
and she hit it hard.

"Go, Zoë!" shouted all the Rockets.

Zoë started to run.

The ball bounced near Luke.
He moved across to catch it,
and Zoë ran onto the base.

"Safe on first base!" called Miss Bell.

All the Rockets had their turn at batting.
The Jets ran after the ball, laughing and shouting.

Then it was the Jets' turn to bat.
Kylie hit the ball across the grass.

"Go, Kylie!" shouted all the Jets,
as she raced past first base.

One by one, the Jets had their turn
until only Luke was left.
He picked up the bat
and looked around the field.
There was someone waiting
on every base.

"The Rockets have 10 runs
and the Jets have 7,"
said Miss Bell.

"You need to hit a home run, Luke!" said Kylie.
"That's the only way we can win."

"I think I can do it," said Luke.

But Luke missed the first two balls.

He held onto the bat tightly,
and watched the last ball
coming towards him.

Then he swung the bat,
and, this time, he hit the ball!

Away it went, up into the air.

Zoë tried to catch the ball,
but it flew over her head.
She chased after it
as it bounced along the grass.

Zoë scooped the ball up,
and started to run with it.

As Luke raced around the bases,
he turned to see who had the ball.

"Keep going, Luke!" shouted the Jets.
"Don't stop!"

"Zoë! Throw the ball to me!" shouted Andrew.

Luke reached third base, and then headed for home.

Luke ran as fast as he could.

Andrew had to move off the base to catch the ball.

"Go, Luke!" shouted the Jets.

"Go, Andrew!" shouted the Rockets.

Then Luke tripped over!

"**Oh, no!**" cried the Jets.

Luke didn't have time to stand up.
He crawled on his hands and knees
to the base, and got there
just before Andrew.

The Jets jumped up and down,
cheering loudly.

"I did it!" puffed Luke.
"We won a game at last!"